Cookies
& Biscuits

THE AUSTRALIAN
Women's Weekly

contents

Imagine the delight I got witnessing this gorgeous book develop! From helping dream up and test the various recipes to seeing them take shape in their amazing photographs, I can't remember when I've had more fun in creating a book. And I know you'll have just as much fun when you bake them at home yourself, a feeling that will only be bettered when you check out the looks on the delighted faces when they first glimpse your cookies.

Pamela Clark

Food Director

There's never been a cookie book like this one — full of fantastic and imaginative ideas that will excite the baker as much as every volunteer taste-tester. The sensationally original creations you'll find here are so versatile they're the perfect gift for the person who has everything as well as being a child's birthday party-stopper. So, who did steal the cookie from the cookie jar?

malted milk numbers

125g butter, softened
½ cup (110g) caster sugar
1 egg
¼ cup (90g) golden syrup
¼ cup (30g) malted milk powder
2½ cups (375g) plain flour
½ teaspoon bicarbonate
   of soda
1½ teaspoons cream of tartar
Lemon icing
1 egg white, beaten lightly
1½ cups (240g) icing sugar
2 teaspoons plain flour
2 teaspoons lemon juice,
   approximately
green food colouring

1 Beat butter, sugar and egg in small bowl with electric mixer until combined. Stir in golden syrup and sifted dry ingredients, in two batches.
2 Knead dough on floured surface until smooth; roll dough between sheets of baking paper until 5mm thick. Refrigerate 30 minutes.
3 Preheat oven to 150°C/130°C fan-forced. Grease oven trays; line with baking paper.
4 Using 6cm number cutters (see page 115), cut 45 numbers from dough; place about 3cm apart on oven trays. Bake about 15 minutes. Cool on trays.
5 Make lemon icing. Spread cookie numbers with icing; set at room temperature.

Lemon icing
Place egg white in small bowl, stir in half the sifted icing sugar, then remaining sifted icing sugar, flour and enough juice to make a thick, spreadable icing. Tint icing green.

Makes 45

0123456789

double chocolate freckles

125g butter, softened
¾ cup (165g) firmly packed
    brown sugar
1 egg
1½ cups (225g) plain flour
¼ cup (35g) self-raising flour
¼ cup (35g) cocoa powder
200g dark eating chocolate,
    melted
⅓ cup (85g) hundreds
    and thousands

1 Beat butter, sugar and egg in small bowl with electric mixer until combined. Stir in sifted dry ingredients, in two batches.
2 Knead dough on floured surface until smooth; roll dough between sheets of baking paper until 5mm thick. Cover; refrigerate 30 minutes.
3 Preheat oven to 180°C/160°C fan-forced. Grease oven trays; line with baking paper.
4 Using 3cm, 5cm and 6.5cm round cutters, cut 14 rounds from dough using each cutter. Place 3cm rounds on one oven tray; place remainder on other oven trays.
5 Bake small cookies about 10 minutes; bake larger cookies about 12 minutes. Cool on wire racks.
6 Spread tops of cookies with chocolate; sprinkle with hundreds and thousands. Set at room temperature.

Makes 42

125g butter, softened
½ cup (110g) caster sugar
1 egg
¼ cup (60ml) golden syrup
2½ cups (375g) plain flour
½ teaspoon bicarbonate of soda
1½ teaspoons cream of tartar
1 teaspoon ground ginger
1 teaspoon ground mixed spice
½ teaspoon ground clove

Pink icing
1 egg white, beaten lightly
1½ cups (240g) icing sugar
2 teaspoons plain flour
2 teaspoons lemon juice,
  approximately
pink food colouring

1 Beat butter, sugar and egg in medium bowl with electric mixer until combined. Stir in syrup and sifted dry ingredients, in two batches.
2 Knead dough on floured surface until smooth; roll dough between sheets of baking paper until 5mm thick. Cover; refrigerate 30 minutes.
3 Preheat oven to 150°C/130°C fan-forced. Grease oven trays; line with baking paper.
4 Using 9cm cross cutter and 7.5cm zero cutter (see page 115), cut shapes from dough. Place about 3cm apart on oven trays.
5 Bake shapes about 15 minutes. Cool on trays.
6 Make pink icing. Spread jumbles with pink icing; set at room temperature

Pink icing
Place egg white in small bowl, stir in half the sifted icing sugar; add remaining sifted icing sugar, flour and enough juice to make a thick spreadable icing. Tint icing pink.

Makes 32

jumble bumbles

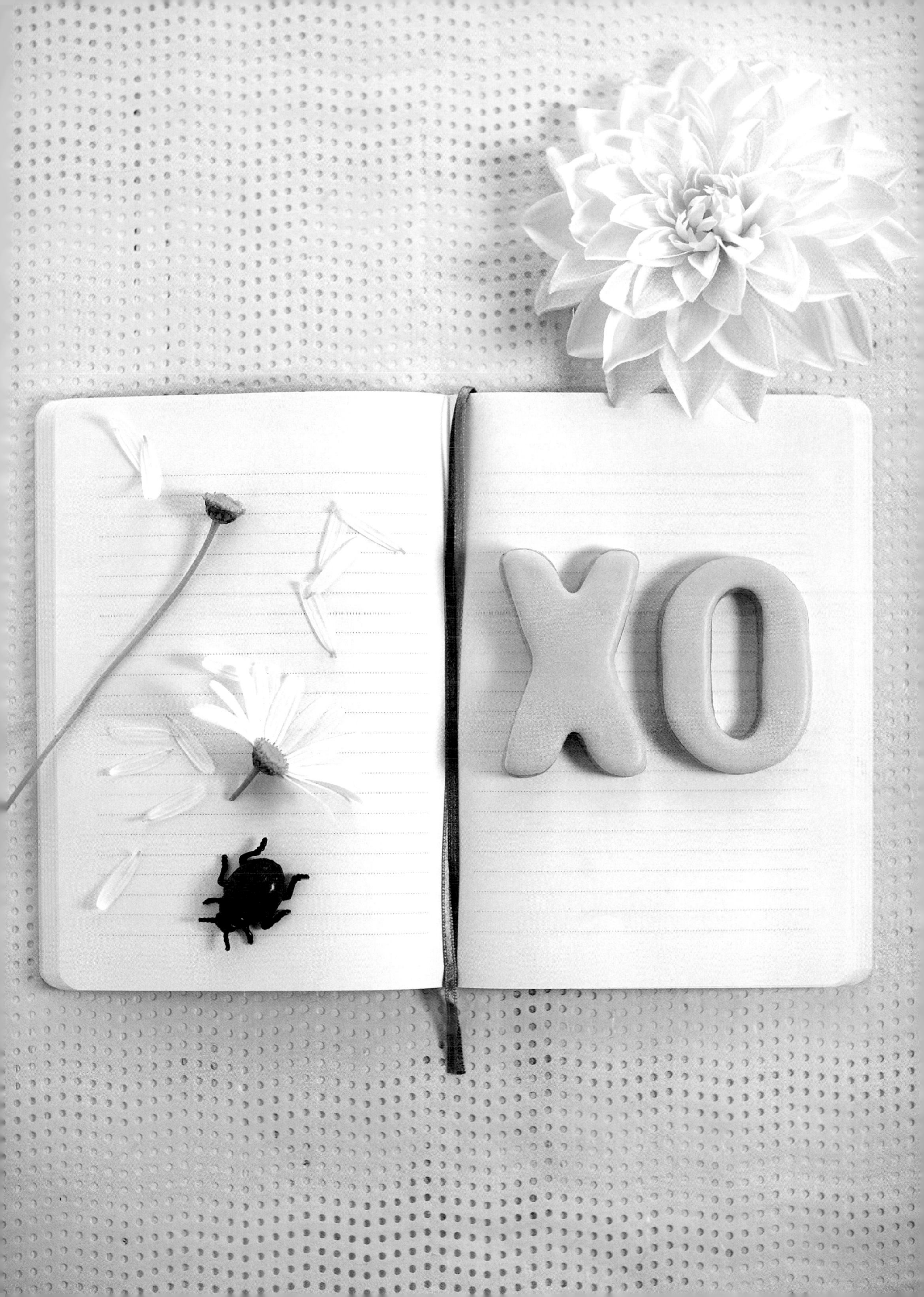
XO

choc-cherry macaroon hearts

100g butter, softened
½ cup (150g) caster sugar
1 egg
2 cups (300g) plain flour
1 tablespoon cocoa powder
100g dark eating chocolate, melted

Macaroon filling
1 egg white
¼ cup (55g) caster sugar
½ teaspoon vanilla extract
¾ cup (60g) desiccated coconut
1 teaspoon plain flour
2 tablespoons finely chopped red glacé cherries

1 Make macaroon filling.
2 Beat butter, sugar and egg in small bowl with electric mixer until light and fluffy; stir in sifted dry ingredients, in two batches. Stir in chocolate.
3 Knead dough on floured surface until smooth. Roll dough between sheets of baking paper until 7mm thick.
4 Preheat oven to 180°C/160°C fan-forced. Grease oven trays; line with baking paper.
5 Using 8cm heart-shaped cutter (see page 115), cut hearts from dough. Place, about 2cm apart, on oven trays. Using 4cm heart-shaped cutter, cut out centres from hearts.
6 Bake cookies about 7 minutes; remove from oven. Reduce oven temperature to 150°C/130°C fan-forced.
7 Divide macaroon mixture among centres of cookies; smooth surface. Cover with foil (like a tent so foil does not touch surface of macaroon). Bake about 15 minutes or until macaroon is firm. Cool on trays 5 minutes; transfer to wire racks to cool.

Macaroon filling
Beat egg white in small bowl with electric mixer until soft peaks form. Gradually add sugar 1 tablespoon at a time, beating until dissolved between additions. Fold in extract, coconut, flour and cherries.

Makes 22

choc-cherry bliss bombs

1⅓ cups (200g) milk chocolate Melts
60g butter
¼ cup (60ml) vegetable oil
⅓ cup (75g) caster sugar
2 eggs
1 cup (150g) self-raising flour
1 cup (150g) plain flour
3 x 55g Cherry Ripe bars, chopped finely
¼ cup (20g) desiccated coconut

1 Stir chocolate, butter, oil and sugar in medium saucepan over low heat until smooth. Cool 15 minutes.
2 Preheat oven to 180°C/160°C fan-forced. Grease oven trays; line with baking paper.
3 Stir eggs and flours into chocolate mixture; stir in Cherry Ripe.
4 Roll level ½ teaspoons of mixture into balls; roll half the balls in coconut. Place about 2cm apart on oven trays.
5 Bake cookies about 10 minutes. Cool on trays.
6 Serve in paper cones (see page 114).

Makes 280

wedding cake cookies

⅓ cup (55g) dried mixed fruit
2 tablespoons brandy
125g butter, softened
1 teaspoon finely grated
orange rind
⅓ cup (75g) caster sugar
1 tablespoon golden syrup
1 cup (150g) self-raising flour
⅔ cup (100g) plain flour
½ teaspoon mixed spice
Fondant icing
300g white prepared fondant,
chopped coarsely
1 egg white
½ teaspoon lemon juice
Royal icing
1½ cups (240g) pure icing sugar
1 egg white

1 Process fruit and brandy until smooth.
2 Beat butter, rind, sugar and syrup in small bowl with electric mixer until combined.
3 Stir in sifted dry ingredients and fruit puree, in two batches.
4 Knead dough on floured surface until smooth; roll dough between sheets of baking paper until 5mm thick. Cover; refrigerate 30 minutes.
5 Preheat oven to 180°C/160°C fan-forced. Grease oven trays; line with baking paper.
6 Using 10.5cm wedding cake cutter (see page 115), cut 12 shapes from dough. Place about 5cm apart on oven trays. Bake about 12 minutes. Cool on wire racks.
7 Make fondant icing. Use a metal spatula, dipped in hot water, to spread icing quickly over cookies; set at room temperature.
8 Make royal icing. Decorate cookies with royal icing.

Fondant icing
Stir fondant in small heatproof bowl over small saucepan of simmering water until smooth. Add egg white and juice; beat until smooth.

Royal icing
Sift icing sugar through fine sieve. Beat egg white until foamy in small bowl with electric mixer; beat in icing sugar, a tablespoon at a time. Cover surface tightly with plastic wrap.

Makes 12

christmas pudding cookies

1⅔ cups (250g) plain flour
⅓ cup (40g) almond meal
⅓ cup (75g) caster sugar
1 teaspoon mixed spice
1 teaspoon vanilla extract
125g cold butter, chopped
2 tablespoons water
700g rich dark fruit cake
⅓ cup (80ml) brandy
1 egg white
400g dark eating chocolate, melted
½ cup (75g) white chocolate Melts, melted
30 red glacé cherries

1 Process flour, meal, sugar, spice, extract and butter until crumbly. Add the water, process until ingredients come together.
2 Knead dough on floured surface until smooth; roll dough between sheets of baking paper until 5mm thick. Cover; refrigerate 30 minutes.
3 Preheat oven to 180°C/160°C fan-forced. Grease oven trays; line with baking paper.
4 Using 5.5cm round cutter (see page 115), cut 30 rounds from dough. Place about 3cm apart on oven trays. Bake about 10 minutes.
5 Meanwhile, crumble fruit cake into a medium bowl; add brandy. Press mixture firmly into round metal tablespoon measures. Brush partially baked cookies with egg white, top with cake domes; bake further 5 minutes. Cool on wire racks.
6 Place wire racks over oven tray, coat cookies with dark chocolate; set at room temperature.
7 Spoon white chocolate over cookies; top with cherries.

Makes 30

coconut fortune cookies

2 egg whites
⅓ cup (75g) caster sugar
⅓ cup (50g) plain flour
1 teaspoon coconut essence
30g butter, melted
½ teaspoon finely grated
    lime rind
2 tablespoons desiccated
    coconut
12 small paper messages

1 Preheat oven to 160°C/140°C fan-forced. Grease oven tray; line with baking paper. Mark two 9cm circles on paper.
2 Beat egg whites in small bowl with electric mixer until soft peaks form; gradually beat in sugar, beating until dissolved between additions.
3 Fold in sifted flour, essence, butter and rind. Drop one level tablespoon of mixture into centre of each circle on oven tray, spread evenly to cover circle completely; sprinkle with a little coconut. Bake about 5 minutes.
4 Working quickly, loosen cookies from tray, place message in the centre of cookies; fold in half then gently bend cookies over edge of a glass (see page 113). Cool 30 seconds. Transfer to wire rack to cool. Repeat with remaining cookie mixture and coconut.

Makes 12

⅔ cup (160ml) passionfruit pulp
¼ cup (55g) finely chopped
  glacé ginger
½ cup (55g) finely chopped
  glacé pineapple
½ cup (90g) finely chopped
  dried papaya
1 cup (75g) shredded coconut
1 cup (60g) coarsely crushed
  cornflakes
½ cup (70g) macadamia nuts,
  chopped finely
¾ cup (180ml) condensed milk
1 cup (150g) white chocolate
  Melts

1 Preheat oven to 180°C/160°C fan-forced. Grease oven trays; line with baking paper.
2 Strain passionfruit pulp; you need ⅓ cup (80ml) juice. Discard seeds.
3 Combine ginger, pineapple, papaya, coconut, cornflakes, nuts, milk and 2 tablespoons of the passionfruit juice in medium bowl.
4 Drop rounded tablespoonfuls of mixture about 5cm apart onto oven trays; press down slightly. Bake about 12 minutes. Cool on trays.
5 Combine chocolate with remaining passionfruit juice in small heatproof bowl; stir over small saucepan of simmering water until smooth. Spread chocolate over flat side of each florentine; mark with a fork. Set at room temperature.

Makes 25

tropical florentines

rhubarb custard melting moments

You need to cook 1 large stem chopped rhubarb with about 1 tablespoon sugar (or to taste) and 1 tablespoon water over low heat, until rhubarb is pulpy Drain, cool.

250g butter, softened
½ teaspoon vanilla extract
½ cup (80g) icing sugar
1 cup (125g) custard powder
1 cup (150g) plain flour
1 tablespoon icing sugar, extra
Rhubarb custard
1 tablespoon custard powder
1 tablespoon caster sugar
½ cup (125ml) milk
⅓ cup stewed rhubarb

1 Preheat oven to 160°C/140°C fan-forced. Grease oven trays; line with baking paper.
2 Make rhubarb custard.
3 Beat butter, extract and sifted icing sugar in small bowl with electric mixer until light and fluffy.
4 Stir in sifted custard powder and flour in two batches.
5 With floured hands, roll rounded teaspoons of mixture into balls. Place about 5cm apart on oven trays; flatten slightly with a floured fork.
6 Bake about 15 minutes. Stand 5 minutes; cool on wire racks.
7 Sandwich biscuits with a little rhubarb custard.

Rhubarb custard
Blend custard powder and sugar with milk in small saucepan; stir over heat until mixture boils and thickens. Remove from heat, stir in rhubarb. Cover surface of custard with plastic wrap; refrigerate until cold.

Makes 25

hot cross bun cookies

125g butter, softened
⅔ cup (150g) caster sugar
1 egg
¼ cup (40g) finely chopped
    mixed peel
½ cup (80g) dried currants
2 cups (300g) self-raising flour
1 teaspoon mixed spice
2 teaspoons milk
2 tablespoons almond meal
100g marzipan
2 tablespoons apricot jam,
    warmed, strained

1 Preheat oven to 160°C/140°C fan-forced. Grease oven trays, line with baking paper.
2 Beat butter, sugar and egg in small bowl with electric mixer until light and fluffy. Stir in peel, currants, sifted flour and spice, and milk in two batches.
3 Roll rounded teaspoons of mixture into balls; place about 5cm apart on oven trays.
4 Knead almond meal into marzipan. Roll marzipan into 5mm diameter sausages; cut into 4cm lengths.
5 Brush cookies with a little milk; place marzipan crosses on cookies, press down gently.
6 Bake about 15 minutes. Brush cookies with jam; cool on trays.

Makes 48

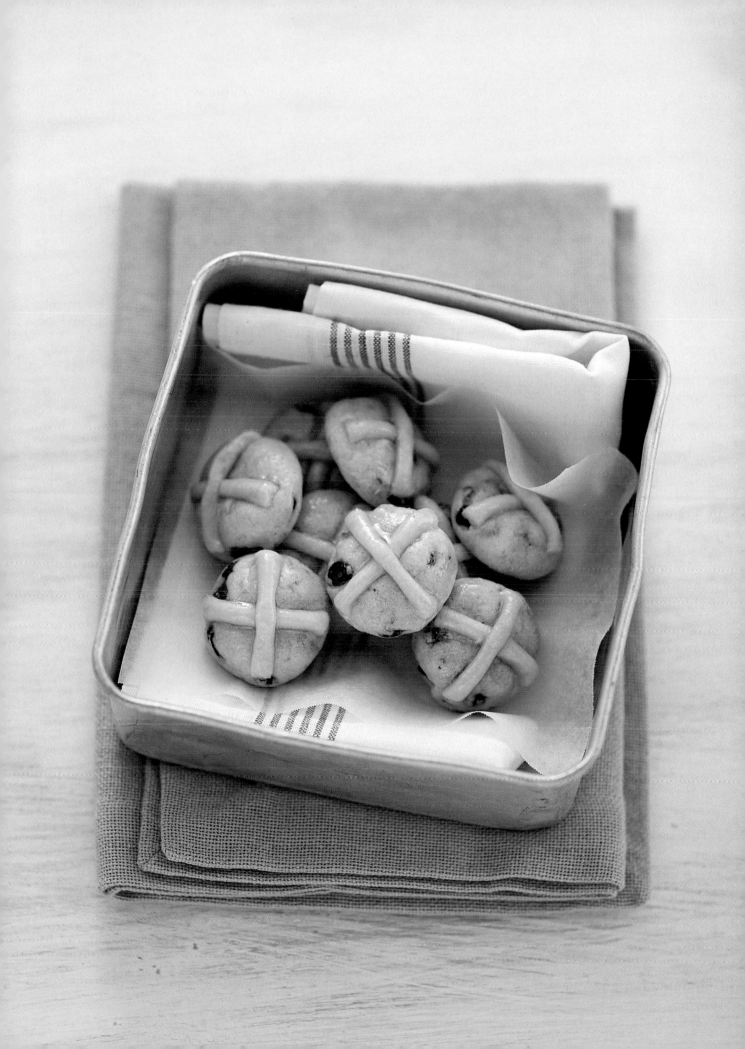

date and walnut scrolls

125g butter, softened
⅓ cup (75g) caster sugar
1 teaspoon ground cardamom
1 egg
1½ cups (225g) plain flour
1 cup (100g) walnuts, roasted,
   ground finely
2 cups (280g) dried dates,
   chopped coarsely
¼ cup (55g) caster sugar, extra
2 teaspoons finely grated
   lemon rind
⅓ cup (80ml) lemon juice
¼ teaspoon ground
   cardamom, extra
½ cup (125ml) water

1 Beat butter, sugar, cardamom and egg in small bowl with electric mixer until combined. Stir in sifted flour and walnuts.
2 Knead dough on floured surface until smooth; divide into two portions. Roll each portion between sheets of baking paper to 15cm x 30cm rectangles; refrigerate 20 minutes.
3 Meanwhile, stir dates, extra sugar, rind, juice, extra cardamom and the water in medium saucepan over heat, without boiling, until sugar is dissolved; bring to a boil. Reduce heat, simmer, uncovered, stirring occasionally, about 5 minutes or until mixture is thick and pulpy. Transfer to large bowl; refrigerate 10 minutes.

4 Spread filling evenly over the two rectangles, leaving 1cm border. Using paper as a guide, roll rectangles tightly from short side to enclose filling. Wrap rolls in baking paper; refrigerate 30 minutes.
5 Preheat oven to 190°C/170°C fan-forced. Grease oven trays; line with baking paper.
6 Trim edges of roll; cut each roll into 1cm slices. Place slices cut-side up on oven trays; bake about 20 minutes.

Makes 28

almond and plum crescents

1½ cups (225g) plain flour
½ cup (60g) almond meal
¼ cup (55g) caster sugar
2 teaspoons finely grated
  lemon rind
90g cream cheese, chopped
90g butter, chopped
2 tablespoons buttermilk
1 egg white
¼ cup (20g) flaked almonds,
  crushed lightly

Filling
⅓ cup (60g) finely chopped
  seeded prunes
¼ cup (80g) plum jam
¼ cup (55g) caster sugar
½ teaspoon ground cinnamon

1 Process flour, almond meal, sugar and rind until combined. Add cream cheese and butter, pulse until crumbly. Add buttermilk, process until ingredients come together.
2 Knead dough on floured surface until smooth. Divide dough in half. Roll each half between sheets of baking paper until large enough to be cut into 22cm rounds; cut dough using 22cm cake pan as a guide. Discard excess dough. Cover rounds; refrigerate 30 minutes.
3 Preheat oven to 180°C/160°C fan-forced. Grease oven trays; line with baking paper.
4 Make filling by combining ingredients in small bowl.
5 Cut each round into eight wedges, spread each wedge with a little filling mixture; roll from the wide end into a crescent shape. Place on oven trays, brush with egg white, sprinkle with flaked almonds. Bake about 25 minutes. Cool on trays.

Makes 16

apple crumble custard creams

1 medium fresh apple (150g), peeled, cored, chopped coarsely
2 teaspoons water
125g butter, softened
⅓ cup (75g) firmly packed brown sugar
2 tablespoons apple concentrate
1 cup (150g) self-raising flour
¾ cup (110g) plain flour
¼ cup (30g) oatbran
¼ cup (20g) desiccated coconut
1 teaspoon ground cinnamon
1 tablespoon icing sugar

Custard cream
1 tablespoon custard powder
1 tablespoon caster sugar
½ cup (125ml) milk
¼ teaspoon vanilla extract
125g cream cheese, softened

1 Stew apple with the water in small saucepan, covered, over medium heat until tender. Mash with a fork; cool.

2 Beat butter, sugar and concentrate in small bowl with electric mixer until combined.

3 Stir in sifted flours, oatbran, stewed apple, coconut and cinnamon, in two batches.

4 Knead dough on floured surface until smooth. Roll dough between sheets of baking paper until 3mm thick; refrigerate 30 minutes.

5 Preheat oven to 180°C/160°C fan-forced. Grease oven trays; line with baking paper.

6 Using 6.5cm apple cutter (see page 115), cut 40 shapes from dough. Place shapes about 3cm apart on oven trays. Bake about 12 minutes. Cool on wire racks.

7 Meanwhile, make custard cream.

8 Sandwich cookies with custard cream. Serve dusted with sifted icing sugar.

Custard cream
Blend custard powder and sugar with milk and extract in small saucepan; stir over heat until mixture boils and thickens. Remove from heat, cover surface with plastic wrap; cool. Beat cream cheese in small bowl with electric mixer until smooth. Add custard; beat until combined.

Makes 20

125g butter, softened
2 teaspoons finely grated
    lemon rind
½ teaspoon almond essence
½ cup (110g) caster sugar
1 egg
1⅔ cups (250g) plain flour
1 egg white
hundreds and thousands
12 paddle pop sticks
180g individually wrapped
    sugar-free fruit drops

1 Beat butter, rind, essence, sugar and egg in small bowl with electric mixer until combined. Stir in sifted flour, in two batches.
2 Knead dough on floured surface until smooth; roll dough between sheets of baking paper until 5mm thick. Cover; refrigerate 30 minutes.
3 Meanwhile, using rolling pin, gently tap wrapped lollies to crush slightly. Unwrap lollies; separate by colour into small bowls.
4 Preheat oven to 180°C/160°C fan-forced. Grease oven trays; line with baking paper.
5 Using 10.5cm round cutter (see page 115), cut 12 rounds from dough. Place about 5cm apart on oven trays.

6 Place 2.5cm, 5cm and 7.5cm cutters starting from the centre of each 10.5cm round. Remove dough between 5cm and 7.5cm cutters; remove dough from centre of 2.5cm cutter (see page 113). Brush half the remaining dough with egg white, sprinkle with hundreds and thousands. Slide one paddle pop stick under each cookie (see page 113).
7 Bake about 10 minutes. Remove trays from oven, fill gaps with crushed lollies; bake further 5 minutes. Cool on trays.

Makes 12

stained-glass lollypops

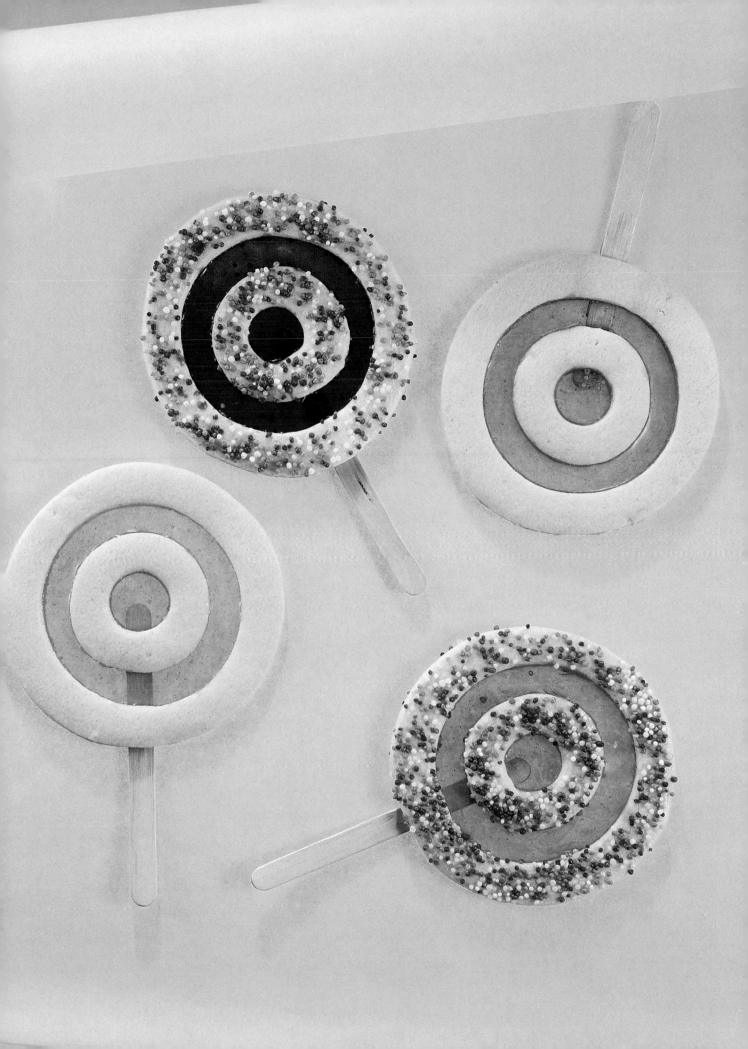

dancing shoes

125g butter, softened
¾ cup (165g) firmly packed
   brown sugar
1 egg
1½ cups (225g) plain flour
¼ cup (35g) self-raising flour
¼ cup (25g) cocoa powder
100g dark eating chocolate,
   melted
silver cachous
Coloured sugar
⅔ cup (150g) caster sugar
pink, yellow, green and purple
   food colouring

1 Beat butter, sugar and egg in small bowl with electric mixer until combined. Stir in sifted flours and cocoa in two batches.
2 Knead dough on floured surface until smooth; roll dough between sheets of baking paper until 5mm thick. Cover; refrigerate 30 minutes.
3 Preheat oven to 180°C/160°C fan-forced. Grease oven trays; line with baking paper.
4 Using a 8.5cm shoe-shaped cutter, cut 25 shapes from dough. Place about 3cm apart on trays. Bake about 12 minutes Cool on trays.
5 Make coloured sugar.
6 Spread cookies with chocolate. Sprinkle shoes with coloured sugar; decorate with cachous.

Coloured sugar
Divide sugar among four small plastic bags. Add different colouring to each bag to tint sugar. Rub colouring into sugar until combined.

Makes 25

ice-cream cones

2 egg whites
⅓ cup (75g) caster sugar
⅓ cup (50g) plain flour
30g butter, melted
½ teaspoon vanilla extract
2 teaspoons cocoa powder
ice-cream

1 Preheat oven to 180°C/160°C fan-forced. Grease oven tray; line with baking paper. Mark a 10cm circle on paper.
2 Beat egg whites in small bowl with electric mixer until soft peaks form; gradually beat in sugar, beating until dissolved between additions. Stir in sifted flour, butter and extract.
3 Place ¼ cup of the mixture in small bowl, stir in sifted cocoa; spoon into a piping bag fitted with a small plain tube.
4 Place a level tablespoon of remaining mixture in centre of each circle on tray, spread evenly to fill circles. Pipe chocolate stripes across circles (see page 111).
5 Bake about 5 minutes. Working quickly, lift cookies from tray, shape into cones (see page 111). Cool on wire racks. Repeat with remaining cookie mixture.
6 Just before serving, fill cookie cones with ice-cream.

Makes 10

50¢

125g butter, softened
2 teaspoons finely grated
orange rind
1 cup (220g) firmly packed
brown sugar
1⅓ cups (200g) wholemeal
self-raising flour
1 cup (100g) walnuts, roasted,
chopped coarsely
⅔ cup (100g) raisins, halved
2 teaspoons dried rosemary
⅓ cup (80ml) orange juice
⅔ cup (50g) desiccated coconut
⅔ cup (60g) rolled oats

1 Preheat oven to 180°C/160°C fan-forced. Grease oven trays; line with baking paper.
2 Beat butter, rind and sugar in small bowl with electric mixer until combined. Transfer to medium bowl; stir in flour then remaining ingredients.
3 Roll rounded tablespoons of mixture into balls, place about 5cm apart on oven trays; flatten slightly. Bake about 15 minutes. Cool on trays.

Makes 28

wholemeal rosemary butter rounds

double choc-chip chilli cookies

250g butter, softened
1 teaspoon vanilla extract
¾ cup (165g) caster sugar
¾ cup (165g) firmly packed
   brown sugar
1 egg
2 cups (300g) plain flour
¼ cup (25g) cocoa powder
1 teaspoon bicarbonate of soda
400g dark eating chocolate,
   chopped coarsely

Candied chillies
¼ cup (55g) caster sugar
¼ cup (60ml) water
3 fresh red thai chillies,
   chopped finely

1 Preheat oven to 180°C/160°C fan-forced. Grease oven trays; line with baking paper.
2 Make candied chillies.
3 Beat butter, extract, sugars and egg in small bowl with electric mixer until light and fluffy; transfer to large bowl.
4 Stir in sifted flour, cocoa and soda in two batches. Stir in chilli and chocolate.
5 Roll level tablespoons of dough into balls; place about 5cm apart on oven trays. Bake about 12 minutes. Cool on trays.

Candied chillies
Stir sugar and the water in small saucepan over heat until sugar dissolves. Add chilli, boil, 2 minutes; cool. Strain, discard syrup.

Makes 48

jammy flowers

125g butter, softened
½ teaspoon vanilla extract
½ cup (110g) caster sugar
1 cup (120g) almond meal
1 egg
1 cup (150g) plain flour
1 teaspoon finely grated
   lemon rind
⅓ cup (110g) raspberry jam
2 tablespoons apricot jam

1 Preheat oven to 180°C/160°C fan-forced. Grease oven trays; line with baking paper.
2 Beat butter, extract, sugar and almond meal in small bowl with electric mixer until light and fluffy. Add egg, beat until combined; stir in sifted flour.
3 Divide rind between both jams; mix well.
4 Roll level tablespoons of mixture into balls; place about 5cm apart on oven trays, flatten slightly. Using end of a wooden spoon, press a flower shape (about 1cm deep) into dough; fill each hole with a little jam, using apricot jam for centres of flowers.
5 Bake about 15 minutes. Cool on trays.

Makes 26

250g butter, softened
1 teaspoon vanilla extract
¾ cup (165g) caster sugar
¾ cup (165g) firmly packed
  brown sugar
1 egg
2 cups (300g) plain flour
¼ cup (25g) cocoa powder
1 teaspoon bicarbonate of soda
⅓ cup (45g) finely chopped
  roasted hazelnuts
⅔ cup (120g) coarsely chopped
  dark eating chocolate
⅔ cup (120g) coarsely chopped
  milk eating chocolate
⅔ cup (120g) coarsely chopped
  white eating chocolate

1 Preheat oven to 180°C/160°C
fan-forced. Grease oven trays;
line with baking paper.
2 Beat butter, extract, sugars and
egg in small bowl with electric
mixer until light and fluffy;
transfer to large bowl.
3 Stir in sifted flour, cocoa and
soda in two batches. Stir in nuts
and chocolate.
4 Roll level tablespoons of
dough into balls; place about
5cm apart on oven trays. Bake
about 12 minutes. Cool on trays.

Makes 48

chocolate fudge brownies

lemon grass, ginger and sesame bars

You will need eight 40g packets of original sesame snaps for this recipe.

125g butter, softened
⅔ cup (130g) firmly packed grated palm sugar
½ teaspoon ground cardamom
½ teaspoon ground cinnamon
pinch ground nutmeg
pinch ground clove
2 egg yolks
1½ cups (225g) plain flour
10cm stick (20g) fresh lemon grass, chopped finely
2 tablespoons finely chopped glacé ginger
32 sesame snaps

1 Beat butter, sugar, spices and egg yolks in small bowl with electric mixer until smooth. Stir in sifted flour, lemon grass and ginger.
2 Knead dough on floured surface until smooth. Roll dough between sheets of baking paper until 5mm thick; refrigerate 30 minutes.
3 Preheat oven to 160°C/140°C fan-forced. Grease oven trays; line with baking paper.
4 Using 9cm square cutter (see page 115), cut 16 shapes from dough; cut in half to make 32 rectangles. Place about 5cm apart on oven trays. Bake 12 minutes.
5 Carefully trim edges of sesame snaps to fit the top of each biscuit. Top each hot biscuit with a sesame snap; bake 3 minutes. Cool on trays.

Makes 32

jigsaw gingerbread people

125g butter, softened
½ cup (110g) firmly packed
   brown sugar
1 egg yolk
2½ cups (375g) plain flour
1 teaspoon bicarbonate of soda
3 teaspoons ground ginger
½ cup (175g) golden syrup
Lemon icing
1 egg white, beaten lightly
1½ cups (240g) icing sugar
2 teaspoons plain flour
2 teaspoons lemon juice,
   approximately
yellow food colouring

1 Preheat oven to 180°C/160°C
fan-forced. Grease oven trays;
line with baking paper.
2 Beat butter, sugar and egg yolk
in small bowl with electric mixer
until smooth; transfer to large
bowl. Stir in sifted dry ingredients
and syrup in two batches.
3 Knead dough on floured
surface until smooth.
4 Divide dough in half; roll each
half between sheets of baking
paper until 5mm thick.
5 Place dough on oven tray.
Using gingerbread people
template (see page 108), cut
around shapes; remove excess
dough (see page 111). Roll
excess dough between sheets
of baking paper until 5mm thick.
Place dough on oven tray. Using
heart template (see page 108),
cut around shape; remove excess
dough (see page 111). Bake
shapes about 15 minutes. Cool
on trays.
6 Make lemon icing. Spread
cookies with icing; set at
room temperature.

Lemon icing
Place egg white in small bowl,
stir in half the sifted icing sugar;
stir in remaining sifted icing
sugar, flour and enough juice to
make a spreadable icing. Tint
icing lemon.

Makes 24 pieces

mud cake sandwiches

250g butter, softened
1½ cups (330g) firmly packed
   brown sugar
2 eggs
3 cups (450g) plain flour
½ cup (75g) self-raising flour
½ cup (50g) cocoa powder
2 tablespoons cocoa
   powder, extra

Chocolate mud cake
150g butter, chopped
100g dark eating chocolate,
   chopped coarsely
1 cup (220g) caster sugar
½ cup (125ml) water
2 tablespoons coffee liqueur
1 cup (150g) plain flour
2 tablespoons cocoa powder
2 egg yolks

Chocolate ganache
⅓ cup (80ml) cream
200g dark eating chocolate,
   chopped coarsely

1 Preheat oven to 170°C/150°C
fan-forced. Grease two 20cm x
30cm lamington pans; line with a
strip of baking paper, extending
paper 2cm above edges of pans.
2 Make chocolate mud cake.
3 Make chocolate ganache.
4 Beat butter, sugar and eggs
in small bowl with electric mixer
until combined. Transfer mixture
to large bowl; stir in sifted flours
and cocoa, in two batches.
Knead dough on floured surface
until smooth; divide in half, roll
each portion between sheets of
baking paper until 5mm thick.
Cover; refrigerate 30 minutes.
5 Preheat oven to 180°C/160°C
fan-forced. Grease oven trays;
line with baking paper.
6 Using 6.5cm round cutter (see
page 115), cut 48 rounds from
dough. Place about 3cm apart
on oven trays. Bake about
12 minutes. Cool on wire racks.
7 Spread ganache onto underside
of cookies; sandwich a mud cake
round between two cookies.
8 Using heart template (see
page 108), dust cookies with
extra cocoa.

Chocolate mud cake
Combine butter, chocolate, sugar,
the water and liqueur in small
saucepan. Stir over low heat until
smooth. Place mixture in medium
bowl; cool 10 minutes. Whisk in
sifted flour and cocoa, then egg
yolks. Divide mixture among
pans. Bake about 25 minutes.
Cool cakes in pans. Using 6.5cm
round cutter (see page 115), cut
12 rounds from each cake.

Chocolate ganache
Bring cream to a boil in small
saucepan; remove from heat.
Add chocolate; stir until smooth.
Refrigerate until spreadable.

Makes 24

chocolate wheaten dominoes

90g butter, softened
½ cup (110g) firmly packed
  brown sugar
1 egg
¼ cup (20g) desiccated
  coconut
¼ cup (25g) wheat germ
¾ cup (120g) wholemeal
  plain flour
⅓ cup (50g) white
  self-raising flour
¼ cup (45g) dark chocolate
  Bits, approximately
150g dark eating chocolate,
  melted

1 Beat butter and sugar in small bowl with electric mixer until smooth; add egg, beat until combined. Stir in coconut, wheat germ and sifted flours.
2 Roll dough between sheets of baking paper until 5mm thick. Cover; refrigerate 30 minutes.
3 Preheat oven to 180°C/160°C fan-forced. Grease oven trays; line with baking paper.
4 Using 9cm square cutter (see page 115), cut 14 squares from dough; cut each square in half to make 28 rectangles. Place about 3cm apart on oven trays. Using a knife, mark (do not cut through) each rectangle across the centre, to make two squares. Press chocolate Bits into each square to make dominoes.
5 Bake about 12 minutes. Cool on trays.
6 Spread bases of dominoes with melted chocolate; set at room temperature on baking-paper-lined oven trays.

Makes 28

lemon-glazed christmas wreaths

3 cups (450g) self-raising flour
125g butter
¼ cup (60ml) milk
⅔ cup (110g) caster sugar
1 teaspoon vanilla extract
2 eggs
silver edible glitter, to decorate
Lemon icing
3 cups (480g) icing sugar
2 tablespoons lemon juice,
  approximately

1 Preheat oven to 180°C/160°C
fan-forced. Grease oven trays;
line with baking paper.
2 Sift flour into medium bowl,
rub in butter. Combine milk and
sugar in small saucepan, stir over
low heat until sugar is dissolved,
add extract; cool 5 minutes. Stir
combined warm milk mixture
and egg into flour mixture.
3 Knead dough on floured
surface until smooth.
4 Roll rounded teaspoons of
dough into 13cm sausages.
Twist two sausages together,
form into circles; press edges
together. Place about 3cm apart
on oven trays.
5 Bake about 15 minutes. Cool
on wire racks.
6 Meanwhile, make lemon icing.
Drizzle wreaths with icing; set at
room temperature. Sprinkle with
edible glitter.

Lemon icing
Sift icing sugar into small
heatproof bowl; stir in enough
juice to make a firm paste.
Stir over small saucepan of
simmering water until pourable.

Makes 30

jaffa jelly cakes

½ cup (110g) caster sugar
2 eggs
1 cup (150g) plain flour
2 tablespoons caster sugar, extra
400g dark eating chocolate,
    melted
3 slices glacé orange,
    cut into wedges

Orange jelly

1 cup (250ml) orange juice
2 tablespoons orange
    marmalade
85g packet orange jelly crystals

1 Make orange jelly.
2 Preheat oven to 180°C/160°C fan-forced. Grease oven trays; line with baking paper.
3 Spread sugar evenly over base of shallow oven tray; heat in oven until sugar feels hot to touch. Beat eggs in small bowl with electric mixer on high speed for 1 minute; add hot sugar, beat about 10 minutes or until mixture is thick and will hold its shape.
4 Meanwhile, sift flour three times. Fit large piping bag with plain 1cm tube.
5 Transfer egg mixture to large bowl, fold in sifted flour. Place mixture into piping bag. Pipe 4cm rounds of mixture onto oven trays, about 3cm apart.
6 Sprinkle each round evenly with extra sugar. Bake each tray, one at a time, about 4 minutes. Cool on trays.
7 Lift jelly from pan to board. Using a 4cm round cutter (see page 115), cut out 25 shapes.
8 Top each sponge with a round of jelly, place on wire rack over tray; coat with chocolate. When chocolate is almost set, top with glacé orange wedges.

Orange jelly

Combine juice and marmalade in small saucepan, bring to a boil; remove from heat. Add jelly crystals, stir until dissolved; cool. Line a deep 23cm-square cake pan with baking paper, extending paper 5cm above edges of pan. Pour jelly into pan; refrigerate until set.

Makes 25

chocolate ginger easter eggs

125g butter, softened
¾ cup (165g) firmly packed
    brown sugar
1 egg
2 tablespoons finely chopped
    glacé ginger
1½ cups (225g) plain flour
¼ cup (35g) self-raising flour
¼ cup (25g) cocoa powder

Chocolate fondant icing
300g chocolate prepared
    fondant, chopped coarsely
1 egg white, beaten lightly

Royal icing
1½ cups (240g) pure icing sugar
1 egg white
pink, green, blue and yellow
    food colouring

1 Beat butter, sugar and egg in small bowl with electric mixer until combined. Stir in ginger then sifted flours and cocoa, in two batches.
2 Knead dough on floured surface until smooth. Roll dough between sheets of baking paper until 5mm thick; refrigerate 30 minutes.
3 Preheat oven to 180°C/160°C fan-forced. Grease oven trays; line with baking paper.
4 Using 2.5cm, 4cm, 5.5cm and 7cm oval cutters (see page 115), cut 13 shapes from dough with each cutter. Place about 3cm apart on oven trays.
5 Bake small cookies about 10 minutes; bake larger cookies about 12 minutes. Cool on wire racks.
6 Make chocolate fondant icing. Use a metal spatula, dipped in hot water, to spread icing quickly over cookies. Set at room temperature.
7 Make royal icing. Divide icing among four bowls. Tint each bowl with food colouring; use to pipe patterns on cookies.

Chocolate fondant icing
Stir fondant in small heatproof bowl over small saucepan of simmering water until smooth. Stir in egg white. Stand at room temperature about 10 minutes or until thickened slightly.

Royal icing
Sift icing sugar through fine sieve. Beat egg white until foamy in small bowl with electric mixer; beat in icing sugar, one tablespoon at a time. Cover surface tightly with plastic wrap.

Makes 52

honey, oat and barley horseshoes

125g butter, softened
½ cup (110g) caster sugar
1 egg
2 tablespoons golden syrup
2 tablespoons honey
½ cup (45g) rolled oats
½ cup (65g) rolled barley
2 cups (300g) plain flour
½ teaspoon bicarbonate of soda
1½ teaspoons cream of tartar
1 teaspoon ground ginger
1 teaspoon mixed spice
½ teaspoon ground clove
½ cup (45g) rolled oats, extra

1 Preheat oven to 180°C/160°C fan-forced. Grease oven trays; line with baking paper.
2 Beat butter, sugar and egg in small bowl with electric mixer until combined. Transfer to large bowl; stir in golden syrup, honey, oats, barley and sifted dry ingredients.
3 Knead dough on floured surface until smooth. Sprinkle surface with extra rolled oats; roll level tablespoons of dough in oats into 12cm sausages.
4 Shape into horseshoe; place about 3cm apart on oven trays. Bake about 20 minutes. Cool on wire racks.

Makes 26

2 x 18g instant latte sachets
1 tablespoon boiling water
125g butter, softened
¾ cup (165g) firmly packed
   brown sugar
1 egg
1½ cups (225g) plain flour
¼ cup (35g) self-raising flour

1 Blend contents of latte sachets with the water in small bowl.
2 Beat butter, sugar, egg and latte paste in small bowl with electric mixer until combined. Stir in sifted flours in two batches.
3 Knead dough on floured surface until smooth; roll dough between sheets of baking paper until 5mm thick. Cover; refrigerate 30 minutes.
4 Preheat oven to 180°C/160°C fan-forced. Grease oven trays; line with baking paper.
5 Using a fancy 7.5cm square cutter (see page 115), cut out 30 squares. Place squares on oven trays. Stamp centre of each cookie with a floured rubber stamp (see pages 108 & 110).
6 Bake about 15 minutes. Cool on wire racks.

Makes 30

girl-about-town latte squares

pink macaroons

3 egg whites
2 tablespoons caster sugar
pink food colouring
1¼ cups (200g) icing sugar
1 cup (120g) almond meal
2 tablespoons icing sugar, extra
White chocolate ganache
100g white eating chocolate,
    chopped coarsely
2 tablespoons thickened cream

1 Make white chocolate ganache.
2 Grease oven trays; line with
baking paper.
3 Beat egg whites in small bowl
with electric mixer until soft
peaks form. Add sugar and
food colouring, beat until sugar
dissolves. Transfer mixture to
large bowl. Fold in sifted icing
sugar and almond meal, in
two batches.
4 Spoon mixture into large
piping bag fitted with 1.5cm
plain tube. Pipe 36 x 4cm
rounds, 2cm apart, onto trays.
Tap trays on bench top to allow
macaroons to spread slightly.
Dust with sifted extra icing sugar;
stand 15 minutes.
5 Preheat oven to 150°C/130°C
fan-forced.
6 Bake macaroons about
20 minutes. Stand 5 minutes;
transfer to wire rack to cool.
7 Sandwich macaroons with
ganache. Dust with a little sifted
icing sugar, if desired.

White chocolate ganache
Stir chocolate and cream in small
saucepan over low heat until
smooth. Transfer mixture to small
bowl. Cover; refrigerate until
mixture is spreadable.

Makes 18

shortbread buttons

250g butter, softened
⅓ cup (75g) caster sugar
¼ cup (35g) rice flour
2¼ cups (335g) plain flour
1 tablespoon caster sugar, extra

1 Preheat oven to 150°C/130°C fan-forced. Grease oven trays; line with baking paper.
2 Beat butter and sugar in small bowl with electric mixer until smooth. Stir in sifted flours. Knead dough on floured surface until smooth.
3 Place 5cm round floured cutter (see page 115) on an oven tray, press one level tablespoon of dough evenly inside the cutter, remove cutter (see page 110). Repeat with remaining dough.
4 Use the lid of a plastic water bottle to indent the buttons. Use a skewer to make holes in buttons. Use a fork to make pattern around edges of buttons (see page 110).
5 Sprinkle buttons with extra sugar. Bake 30 minutes or until firm. Cool on trays.

Makes 26

caramel ginger crunchies

2 cups (300g) plain flour
½ teaspoon bicarbonate of soda
1 teaspoon ground cinnamon
2 teaspoons ground ginger
1 cup (220g) caster sugar
125g cold butter, chopped
1 egg
1 teaspoon golden syrup
2 tablespoons finely chopped
   glacé ginger
45 wrapped hard caramels

1 Preheat oven to 160°C/140°C fan-forced. Grease oven trays; line with baking paper.
2 Process sifted dry ingredients with butter until mixture is crumbly; add egg, golden syrup and ginger, process until ingredients come together. Knead on floured surface until smooth.
3 Roll rounded teaspoons of mixture into balls; flatten slightly. Place about 3cm apart on oven trays.
4 Bake 13 minutes. Place one caramel on top of each hot cookie. Bake about 7 minutes or until caramel begins to melt. Cool on trays.

Makes 45

christmas angels

125g butter, softened
¾ cup (165g) caster sugar
1 egg
1½ cups (225g) plain flour
¼ cup (35g) self-raising flour
½ cup (40g) desiccated coconut
⅓ cup (110g) apricot jam,
  warmed, strained
Macaroon topping
3 egg whites
¾ cup (165g) caster sugar
¼ cup (35g) plain flour
2¼ cups (180g) desiccated
  coconut

1 Beat butter, sugar and egg in small bowl with electric mixer until light and fluffy. Stir in sifted flours and coconut in two batches.
2 Knead dough on floured surface until smooth; roll dough between sheets of baking paper until 5mm thick. Cover; refrigerate 30 minutes.
3 Preheat oven to 180°C/160°C fan-forced. Grease oven trays; line with baking paper.
4 Make macaroon topping.
5 Using 11cm angel cutter (see page 115), cut 16 angel shapes from dough. Place, about 3cm apart, on oven trays.
6 Bake 8 minutes. Spread each hot cookie with jam; divide macaroon topping among angels. Cover with foil (like a tent so foil does not touch surface of macaroon). Bake about 7 minutes. Cool on wire racks.

Macaroon topping
Beat egg whites in small bowl with electric mixer until soft peaks form. Gradually add sugar, beating until dissolved between additions. Fold in sifted flour and coconut in two batches.

Makes 16

green tea and almond tiles

125g butter, softened
¼ cup (55g) caster sugar
½ teaspoon vanilla extract
1 egg
1 cup (150g) plain flour
2 tablespoons self-raising flour
¼ cup (35g) cornflour
1 tablespoon green tea leaves
  (about 4 tea bags)
½ cup (60g) almond meal

Fondant icing
300g white prepared fondant,
  chopped coarsely
1 egg white, beaten lightly

Royal icing
1½ cups (240g) pure icing sugar
1 egg white
½ teaspoon vanilla extract
black food colouring

1 Beat butter, sugar, extract and egg in small bowl with electric mixer until light and fluffy. Stir in sifted flours, tea and almond meal.
2 Knead dough on floured surface until smooth; roll dough between sheets of baking paper until 5mm thick. Cover, refrigerate 30 minutes.
3 Preheat oven to 180°C/160°C fan-forced. Grease oven trays; line with baking paper.
4 Using 9.5cm square cutter (see page 115), cut 14 squares from dough. Cut squares in half to make 28 rectangles. Place about 3cm apart on oven trays.
5 Bake about 15 minutes. Cool on wire racks.
6 Make fondant icing. Make royal icing.
7 Using a metal spatula dipped in hot water, spread cookies with fondant icing. Decorate with black royal icing.

Fondant icing
Stir fondant in small heatproof bowl over small saucepan of simmering water until smooth. Add egg white; stir until smooth.

Royal icing
Sift icing sugar through fine sieve. Beat egg white until foamy in small bowl with electric mixer; add icing sugar, a tablespoon at a time. When icing reaches firm peaks, use a wooden spoon to beat in extract and colouring; cover surface tightly with plastic wrap.

Makes 28

frangipanis

185g butter, softened
1 teaspoon coconut essence
2 teaspoons finely grated
   lime rind
⅓ cup (75g) caster sugar
1½ cups (225g) plain flour
¼ cup (35g) rice flour
⅓ cup (30g) desiccated coconut
¼ cup (55g) finely chopped
   glacé pineapple
1 tablespoon purple
   coloured sprinkles
Fondant icing
300g white prepared fondant,
   chopped coarsely
1 egg white, beaten lightly
pink food colouring

1 Beat butter, essence, rind and sugar in small bowl with electric mixer until smooth. Stir in sifted flours, coconut and pineapple in two batches.
2 Knead dough on floured surface until smooth. Roll dough between sheets of baking paper until 5mm thick. Refrigerate 30 minutes.
3 Preheat oven to 160°C/140°C fan-forced. Grease round based patty pans (see page 108).
4 Using 7cm flower cutter (see page 115), cut 28 shapes from dough. Place in patty pans (see page 114).
5 Bake about 10 minutes. Cool in pans.
6 Make fondant icing. Using a metal spatula dipped in hot water, spread pink icing quickly over cookies. Sprinkle coloured sprinkles into centres of flowers.

Fondant icing
Stir fondant in small bowl over small saucepan of simmering water until smooth. Add egg white; stir until smooth. Tint with colouring.

Makes 28

iced marshmallow butterflies

You will need three 250g packets raspberry and vanilla marshmallows for this recipe.

125g butter, softened
¾ cup (165g) caster sugar
1 egg
1½ cups (225g) plain flour
¼ cup (35g) self-raising flour
½ cup (40g) desiccated coconut
⅓ cup (25g) desiccated coconut, extra
Topping
¼ cup (80g) strawberry jam, warmed, strained, cooled
48 pink marshmallows, quartered
48 white marshmallows, quartered

1 Beat butter, sugar and egg in small bowl with electric mixer until light and fluffy. Stir in sifted flours and coconut, in two batches.
2 Knead dough on floured surface until smooth. Roll dough between sheets of baking paper until 5mm thick; refrigerate 30 minutes.
3 Preheat oven to 180°C/160°C fan-forced. Grease oven trays; line with baking paper.
4 Using 11.5cm butterfly cutter (see page 115), cut 16 shapes from dough. Place about 3cm apart on oven trays. Bake about 12 minutes.
5 Meanwhile, using scissors, quarter marshmallows. Press marshmallows cut-side down onto hot butterfly wings, trim marshmallows to the shape of the wings if necessary. Brush marshmallows with a little water; sprinkle with extra coconut. Bake about 1 minute or until marshmallows soften slightly.
6 Pipe jam down centre of each butterfly. Cool on wire racks.

Makes 16

hazelnut chai teacups

125g butter, softened
1 teaspoon vanilla extract
¼ cup (55g) caster sugar
1 egg yolk
1 cup (150g) plain flour
2 tablespoons self-raising flour
¼ cup (35g) cornflour
1 tablespoon chai tea
(about 4 chai tea bags)
½ cup (50g) hazelnut meal

Fondant icing

300g white prepared fondant,
chopped coarsely
1 egg white, beaten lightly
1 teaspoon lemon juice
yellow, blue and green
food colouring

Royal icing

1½ cups (240g) pure icing sugar
1 egg white

1 Preheat oven to 180°C/160°C fan-forced. Grease oven trays; line with baking paper.

2 Beat butter, extract, sugar and egg yolk in small bowl with electric mixer until light and fluffy. Stir in sifted flours, tea and hazelnut meal.

3 Knead dough on floured surface until smooth; roll dough between sheets of baking paper until 5mm thick.

4 Using 8.5cm teacup cutter, cut out 14 shapes from dough. Place about 3cm apart on oven trays. Bake about 15 minutes. Cool on trays.

5 Make fondant icing. Using a metal spatula dipped in hot water, spread icing quickly over cookies.

6 Make royal icing. Decorate cookies with royal icing.

Fondant icing

Stir fondant in small heatproof bowl over small saucepan of simmering water until smooth; stir in egg white and juice. Divide among three bowls; tint yellow, blue and green with food colouring.

Royal icing

Sift icing sugar through fine sieve. Beat egg white until foamy in small bowl with electric mixer; beat in icing sugar a tablespoon at a time. Cover surface tightly with plastic wrap.

Makes 14

hazelnut shortbread trees

250g butter, softened
2 teaspoons finely grated
   orange rind
½ cup (80g) icing sugar
2 tablespoons rice flour
2 cups (300g) plain flour
2 teaspoons mixed spice
¼ cup (75ml) hazelnut meal
silver cachous
1 tablespoon icing sugar, extra

Brandy butter cream
60g butter, softened
½ teaspoon finely grated
   orange rind
¾ cup (120g) icing sugar
2 teaspoons brandy

1 Beat butter, rind and sifted icing sugar in small bowl with electric mixer until light and fluffy. Transfer to large bowl. Stir in sifted flours and spice, and hazelnut meal, in two batches.
2 Knead dough on floured surface until smooth. Roll dough between sheets of baking paper until 5mm thick; refrigerate 30 minutes.
3 Preheat oven to 180°C/160°C fan-forced. Grease oven trays; line with baking paper.
4 Using 3cm, 5cm and 7cm star-shaped cutters (see page 115), cut 24 of each size star from dough. Place small stars, about 1cm apart, on an oven tray; place remaining stars, about 2cm apart, on oven trays.
5 Bake small stars about 10 minutes. Bake larger stars about 15 minutes. Stand 5 minutes; cool on wire racks.
6 Meanwhile, make brandy butter cream.

7 Sandwich two of each size cookie with butter cream. Assemble trees by joining three different size stars together with butter cream.
8 Decorate trees by joining cachous to stars with a tiny dot of butter cream. Dust trees with extra sifted icing sugar.

Brandy butter cream
Beat butter, rind, sifted icing sugar and brandy in small bowl with electric mixer until light and fluffy.

Makes 12

chocolate and craisin checkerboards

200g butter, softened
¾ cup (165g) caster sugar
½ teaspoon vanilla extract
1 egg
2 cups (300g) plain flour
1 tablespoon cocoa powder
1 teaspoon finely grated
  orange rind
¼ cup (40g) finely
  chopped craisins
1 egg white, beaten lightly

1 Beat butter, sugar, extract and egg in small bowl with electric mixer until light and fluffy. Stir in sifted flour in two batches.
2 Divide dough in half, knead sifted cocoa into one half; knead rind and craisins into the other half. Using ruler, shape each batch of dough into 4.5cm x 4.5cm x 15cm rectangular bars (see page 112). Wrap each in baking paper; refrigerate 30 minutes.
3 Cut each bar lengthways equally into three slices. Cut each slice lengthways equally into three; you will have nine 1.5cm x 1.5cm x 1.5cm slices of each dough (see page 112).
4 Brush each slice of dough with egg white, stack alternate flavours together in threes. Stick three stacks together to recreate the log (see page 112); repeat with second log. Refrigerate 30 minutes.

5 Preheat oven to 180°C/160°C fan-forced. Grease oven trays; line with baking paper.
6 Using a sharp knife, cut each log into 1cm slices (see page 112). Place, cut-side up, on oven trays about 3cm apart. Bake about 15 minutes. Stand 5 minutes before lifting onto wire racks to cool.

Makes 30

baby shapes

125g butter, softened
2 teaspoons finely grated
   orange rind
¼ cup (55g) caster sugar
1 egg yolk
1 cup (150g) plain flour
2 tablespoons self-raising flour
¼ cup (35g) cornflour
½ cup (60g) almond meal
1 tablespoon finely chopped
   dried lavender or dried
   rose buds
Lemon icing
1 egg white
1½ cups (240g) icing sugar
2 teaspoons plain flour
2 teaspoons lemon juice,
   approximately
blue food colouring
Royal icing
1½ cups (240g) pure icing sugar
1 egg white
blue food colouring

1 Beat butter, rind, sugar and egg yolk in small bowl with electric mixer until light and fluffy. Stir in sifted flours, almond meal and lavender or rose.
2 Knead dough on floured surface until smooth; roll between sheets of baking paper until 5mm thick. Cover; refrigerate 30 minutes.
3 Preheat oven to 180°C/160°C fan-forced. Grease oven trays; line with baking paper.
4 Using 12.5cm bottle and 11cm pram cutters (see page 115), cut 7 shapes of each from dough. Place about 3cm apart on oven trays.
5 Bake about 12 minutes. Cool on trays.
6 Make lemon icing; spread icing evenly over cookies.
7 Make royal icing. Decorate cookies with royal icing.

Lemon icing
Place egg white in small bowl, stir in half the sifted icing sugar; stir in remaining sifted icing sugar, flour and enough juice to make a thick, spreadable icing. Divide icing among two bowls; tint one bowl with blue food colouring.

Royal icing
Sift icing sugar through fine sieve. Beat egg white until foamy in small bowl with electric mixer; beat in icing sugar a tablespoon at a time. Divide icing among two bowls; tint one bowl with blue food colouring. Cover surface of icing tightly with plastic wrap.

Makes 14

choc-mallow wheels

You will need a 250g packet of raspberry and vanilla marshmallows for this recipe.

125g butter, softened
¾ cup (165g) firmly packed
   brown sugar
1 egg
1½ cups (225g) plain flour
¼ cup (35g) self-raising flour
¼ cup (25g) cocoa powder
28 marshmallows
¼ cup (80g) raspberry jam
375g dark chocolate Melts
1 tablespoon vegetable oil

1 Beat butter, sugar and egg in small bowl with electric mixer until combined. Stir in sifted flours and cocoa, in two batches.
2 Knead dough on floured surface until smooth. Roll between sheets of baking paper until 3mm thick. Cover; refrigerate 30 minutes.
3 Preheat oven to 180°C/160°C fan-forced. Grease oven trays; line with baking paper.
4 Using 7cm round fluted cutter, cut 28 rounds from dough. Place about 3cm apart on trays.
5 Bake about 12 minutes. Cool on wire racks.
6 Turn half the biscuits base-side up; place on oven tray. Use scissors to cut marshmallows in half horizontally. Press four marshmallow halves, cut-side down, onto biscuit bases on tray. Bake 2 minutes.

7 Melt chocolate in medium heatproof bowl over medium saucepan of simmering water. Remove from heat; stir in oil.
8 Spread jam over bases of remaining cookies; press onto softened marshmallow. Stand 20 minutes or until marshmallow is firm. Dip wheels into chocolate; smooth away excess chocolate using metal spatula. Place on baking-paper-lined trays to set.

Makes 14

passionfruit gems

1 cup (150g) plain flour
½ cup (75g) self-raising flour
2 tablespoons custard powder
⅔ cup (110g) icing sugar
90g cold butter, chopped
1 egg yolk
¼ cup (60ml) passionfruit pulp

Butter icing
125g unsalted butter, softened
1½ cups (240g) icing sugar
2 tablespoons milk

1 Process dry ingredients and butter together until crumbly; add egg yolk and passionfruit pulp, pulse until ingredients come together.
2 Knead dough on floured surface until smooth. Roll between sheets of baking paper until 5mm thick; refrigerate 30 minutes.
3 Preheat oven to 180°C/160°C fan-forced. Grease oven trays; line with baking paper.
4 Using 4cm round flower-shaped cutter (see page 115), cut rounds from dough. Place about 3cm apart on oven trays.
5 Bake about 10 minutes. Cool on wire racks.
6 Make butter icing.
7 Spoon icing into piping bag fitted with a small fluted tube. Pipe stars onto cookies.

Butter icing
Beat butter in small bowl with electric mixer until as white as possible. Gradually beat in half the sifted icing sugar, milk, then remaining icing sugar.

Makes 70

slice and bake cookies

250g butter, softened
1¼ cups (200g) icing sugar
1 teaspoon vanilla extract
2 cups (300g) plain flour
½ cup (75g) rice flour
⅓ cup (50g) cornflour
2 tablespoons milk

1 Beat butter, sifted icing sugar and extract in small bowl with electric mixer until light and fluffy. Transfer to large bowl; stir in sifted flours, in two batches, then milk.
2 Divide mixture in half. Knead each half on floured surface until smooth, then roll each half into 25cm logs. Wrap each log in baking paper; refrigerate about 1 hour or until firm.
3 Preheat oven to 160°C/140°C fan-forced. Grease oven trays; line with baking paper.
4 Cut the logs into 1cm slices; place about 3cm apart on oven trays. Bake about 20 minutes. Cool on wire racks.

Makes 48

Variations

Orange and poppy seed
Omit vanilla extract; beat 1 tablespoon finely grated orange rind with butter and sugar. Add 2 tablespoons poppy seeds with sifted flours.

Lemon and craisin
Omit vanilla extract; beat 1 tablespoon finely grated lemon rind with butter and sugar. Stir in ¾ cup (100g) coarsely chopped craisins with sifted flours.

Pecan and cinnamon
Add 1 teaspoon ground cinnamon to sifted flours, then stir in 1 cup (120g) coarsely chopped pecans. Sprinkle with cinnamon sugar before baking.

M&M's
Stir in 2 x 35g packets of mini M&M's with sifted flours.

coffee walnut creams

1⅔ cups (250g) plain flour
125g cold butter, chopped
¼ cup (55g) caster sugar
½ teaspoon vanilla extract
1 egg, beaten lightly
18 walnut halves

Walnut butter cream
185g unsalted butter, softened
¾ cup (120g) icing sugar
1 tablespoon cocoa
1 tablespoon instant
    coffee granules
1 tablespoon hot water
1¼ cups (125g) walnuts,
    chopped finely

Coffee icing
1 cup (160g) icing sugar
2 teaspoons instant
    coffee granules
1 tablespoon hot water
1 teaspoon butter

1 Sift flour into medium bowl, rub in butter. Stir in sugar, extract and egg.
2 Knead dough on floured surface until smooth. Divide in half. Roll, in half between sheets of baking paper until 3mm thick. Refrigerate 30 minutes.
3 Preheat oven to 180°C/160°C fan-forced. Grease oven trays; line with baking paper.
4 Using 5.5cm round cutter (see page 115), cut out 36 rounds. Place on oven trays; bake about 12 minutes. Cool on wire racks.
5 Meanwhile, make walnut butter cream.
6 Sandwich cookies with butter cream; refrigerate 30 minutes.
7 Meanwhile, make coffee icing.
8 Spread cookies with icing and top with walnut halves.

Walnut butter cream
Beat butter and sifted icing sugar in small bowl with electric mixer until light and fluffy. Beat in combined cocoa, coffee and the water. Stir in nuts.

Coffee icing
Sift icing sugar into small heatproof bowl, stir in combined coffee and the water; add butter. Stir over small saucepan of simmering water until icing is spreadable.

Makes 18

nutty meringue sticks

3 egg whites
¾ cup (165g) caster sugar
1¼ cups (120g) hazelnut meal
1½ cups (185g) almond meal
¼ cup (35g) plain flour
100g dark eating chocolate,
  melted

1 Preheat oven to 160°C/140°C fan-forced. Grease oven trays; line with baking paper.
2 Beat egg whites in small bowl with electric mixer until foamy. Gradually beat in sugar, one tablespoon at a time, until dissolved between additions. Transfer mixture to large bowl.
3 Fold in nut meals and sifted flour. Spoon mixture into large piping bag fitted with 1.5cm plain tube. Pipe 8cm sticks onto trays.
4 Bake about 15 minutes. Cool on trays 5 minutes; place on wire racks to cool.
5 Drizzle sticks with melted chocolate, place on baking-paper-lined trays to set.

Makes 34

pistachio shortbread mounds

⅔ cup (70g) shelled
   pistachios, roasted
250g butter, softened
1 cup (160g) icing sugar
1½ cups (225g) plain flour
2 tablespoons rice flour
2 tablespoons cornflour
¾ cup (90g) almond meal
⅓ cup (55g) icing sugar, extra

1 Preheat oven to 150°C/130°C fan-forced. Grease oven trays; line with baking paper.
2 Coarsely chop half the nuts.
3 Beat butter and sifted icing sugar in small bowl with electric mixer until light and fluffy; transfer to large bowl. Stir in sifted flours, almond meal and chopped nuts.
4 Shape level tablespoons of mixture into mounds; place about 3cm apart on oven trays. Press one whole nut on each mound; bake about 25 minutes. Stand 5 minutes; place on wire racks to cool. Serve dusted with extra sifted icing sugar.

Makes 35

chocolate lady's kisses

80g butter, softened
½ teaspoon vanilla extract
¼ cup (55g) caster sugar
1 egg
½ cup (50g) hazelnut meal
¾ cup (110g) plain flour
¼ cup (25g) cocoa powder
1 tablespoon cocoa powder, extra
Choc-hazelnut cream
100g dark eating chocolate,
    melted
50g butter
⅓ cup (110g) chocolate
    hazelnut spread

1 Beat butter, extract, sugar and egg in small bowl with electric mixer until combined. Stir in hazelnut meal, then sifted flour and cocoa.
2 Roll dough between sheets of baking paper until 3mm thick. Refrigerate 1 hour.
3 Make choc-hazelnut cream.
4 Preheat oven to 180°C/160°C fan-forced. Grease oven trays; line with baking paper.
5 Using 4cm fluted cutter, cut 52 rounds from dough. Place on oven trays.
6 Bake about 8 minutes. Stand 5 minutes; place on wire racks to cool.
7 Spoon choc hazelnut cream into piping bag fitted with large fluted tube. Pipe cream onto one biscuit; top with another biscuit. Repeat with remaining biscuits and cream. Dust with extra sifted cocoa.

Choc-hazelnut cream
Beat cooled chocolate, butter and spread in small bowl with electric mixer until thick and glossy.

Makes 26

250g butter, softened
1 teaspoon vanilla extract
½ cup (110g) firmly packed
   brown sugar
1 cup (220g) caster sugar
2 eggs
2¾ cups (410g) plain flour
1 teaspoon bicarbonate of soda
½ teaspoon ground nutmeg
1 tablespoon caster sugar, extra
2 teaspoons ground cinnamon

1 Beat butter, extract and sugars in small bowl with electric mixer until light and fluffy. Add eggs, one at a time, beating until combined. Transfer to large bowl.
2 Stir in sifted flour, soda and nutmeg, in two batches. Cover; refrigerate 30 minutes.
3 Preheat oven to 180°C/160°C fan-forced. Grease oven trays; line with baking paper.
4 Combine extra caster sugar and cinnamon in small shallow bowl. Roll level tablespoons of the dough into balls; roll balls in cinnamon sugar. Place balls about 7cm apart on oven trays.
5 Bake about 12 minutes. Cool on trays.

Makes 42

snickerdoodles

praline custard creams

1 cup (150g) plain flour
1¼ cups (90g) almond meal
90g cold butter, chopped
1 egg yolk
1 teaspoon vanilla extract
2 tablespoons icing sugar

Custard filling
⅓ cup (75g) caster sugar
¼ cup (35g) plain flour
2 egg yolks
1 cup (250ml) milk
125g butter, softened
1 teaspoon vanilla extract
½ cup (80g) icing sugar

Almond praline
½ cup (40g) flaked almonds
½ cup (110g) caster sugar
2 tablespoons water

1 Make custard filling and almond praline.
2 Preheat oven to 160°C/140°C fan-forced. Grease oven trays; line with baking paper.
3 Process flour, meal and butter until crumbly. Add egg yolk and extract; pulse until combined.
4 Knead dough on floured surface until smooth. Roll dough between sheets of baking paper until 3mm thick.
5 Using 3.5cm round cutter (see page 115), cut 72 rounds from dough. Place about 2cm apart on oven trays. Bake about 12 minutes. Cool on trays.
6 Sandwich cookies with custard filling. Spread a little more custard filling around side of cookies. Roll cookies in praline then dust with sifted icing sugar.

Custard filling
Combine sugar and flour in small saucepan; gradually stir in combined yolks and milk until smooth. Cook, stirring, until mixture boils and thickens. Simmer, stirring, over low heat, 1 minute; remove from heat. Cover surface of custard with plastic wrap; refrigerate until cold. Beat butter and extract until mixture is as white as possible. Beat in sifted icing sugar. Beat in cooled custard, in four batches, until smooth.

Almond praline
Place nuts on baking-paper-lined oven tray. Combine sugar and the water in small fying pan; stir over heat, without boiling, until sugar is dissolved. Bring to a boil, boil, uncovered, without stirring, until golden brown. Pour toffee over nuts; set at room temperature. Crush praline finely in food processor.

Makes 36

choconut mint stacks

You will need four 125g packets of After Dinner Mints for this recipe.

125g butter, softened
¾ cup (165g) firmly packed
  brown sugar
1 egg
1½ cups (225g) plain flour
¼ cup (35g) self-raising flour
2 tablespoons desiccated
  coconut
½ teaspoon coconut essence
2 tablespoons cocoa powder
40 square After Dinner Mints

1 Beat butter, sugar and egg in small bowl with electric mixer until combined. Stir in sifted flours in two batches. Place half the mixture into another small bowl; stir in coconut and essence. Stir sifted cocoa into the other bowl.
2 Knead each portion of dough on floured surface until smooth. Roll between sheets of baking paper until 3mm thick. Cover; refrigerate 30 minutes.
3 Preheat oven to 180°C/160°C fan-forced. Grease oven trays; line with baking paper.
4 Using 6cm square cutter (see page 115), cut 30 shapes from each portion of dough. Place about 3cm apart on oven trays.
5 Bake about 8 minutes. While cookies are still hot, sandwich three warm alternate-flavoured cookies with After Dinner Mints; press down gently. Cool on trays.

Makes 20

equipment

1. Piping bags
Available in various sizes from chefs' supply shops and cookware shops, these are usually made from a waterproof fabric. Bags can also be made from baking or greaseproof paper (see page 114); ideal for small amounts of icing.

2. Round-based patty pan
Ideal for drying flowers, leaves etc (see page 114). Available from some supermarkets and cookware shops.

3. Plastic ruler
Used for measuring and straightening edges of dough in Chocolate and craisin checkerboards, page 85.

4. Heart template
Used as a template in Mud cake sandwiches, page 53 (see also page 110).

5. Stamps
Available from craft shops in many shapes and sizes. Used in Girl-about-town latte squares, page 65 (see also page 110).

6. Plastic icing tubes
Can be bought from cake decorating suppliers, some craft shops, supermarkets and cookware shops.

7. Gingerbread people template
Available from craft shops. Used as a template in Jigsaw gingerbread people, page 50 (see also page 111).

8. Rolling pin, spoon and brush
All available from cookware shops, some supermarkets and department stores.

9. Metal spatula
Available in various sizes from cookware shops, chefs' supply shops some supermarkets and department stores.

10. Paddle pop sticks and skewers
Paddle pop sticks can be bought from supermarkets and craft stores. Bamboo skewers can be bought from most supermarkets and cookware shops.

11. Measuring spoons
Can be bought from supermarkets, chain stores and cookware shops.

12. Baking paper
Used for making piping bags, lining oven trays and cake pans. Available from supermarkets and cookware stores.

13. Colourings
Many types are available from cake decorating suppliers, craft shops and some supermarkets; all are concentrated. Use a minute amount of any type of colouring first to determine its strength.

14. Strainer and edible glitter
Fine strainers are essential for sifting pure icing sugar. Edible glitter is available from cake decorating suppliers.

15. Oven tray and wire rack
Available from supermarkets, chain stores and cookware shops.

Shortbread buttons, page 69

To make neat buttons, place 5cm round floured cutter on baking-paper-lined oven tray. Using a small teaspoon, press one level tablespoon of dough evenly inside the cutter. Remove cutter, wipe, dip in flour again, repeat with remaining dough.

To mark indented centres of buttons, use the lid of a plastic water bottle, dipped in flour. Mark holes in buttons using a bamboo skewer or knitting needle. Use a floured fork to gently mark pattern around edges of buttons.

Girl-about-town latte squares, page 65

To mark the squares clearly, use well-defined stamps such as high-heeled shoes, lips, handbags etc. Dip the stamps in flour, shake away any excess, then use to mark the squares of dough. Be sure to keep the stamps clean and re-flour between each use.

Mud cake sandwiches, page 53

Make a heart-shaped template from light cardboard, large enough to completely cover the top of the sandwiches. Place cocoa into a fine sieve, shake into the heart shape. Carefully remove template. Repeat with the remaining sandwiches.

cookie-making tips

Jigsaw gingerbread people, page 50
Cut out paper shapes from template (see page 108). Place half the rolled out dough, still on its baking paper, onto an oven tray, position paper cut-outs from the template on the dough. Using sharp pointed vegetable knife, carefully cut around the shapes.

Carefully pull excess dough away from jigsaw shapes. Gently knead scraps of dough together on lightly floured surface. Re-roll dough between sheets of baking paper to make more jigsaw shapes.

Ice-cream cones, page 38
Spread one level tablespoon of the plain mixture into the marked circles on the baking-paper-lined oven trays. Fill a paper piping bag (see page 114) with chocolate mixture, snip end of bag, pipe chocolate stripes across the circles.

As soon as shapes feel slightly firm (not crisp) in the oven, remove the tray from the oven. Working quickly, slide a knife or spatula blade under each shape to loosen; twist each circle into a cone shape. Place on a wire rack to cool completely.

Chocolate and craisin checkerboards, page 85
Using the side of a plastic ruler, push and shape each piece of dough into the same size rectangular bar shape. Make sure all the sides of both bars are the same height, depth and width. Wrap each bar in baking paper; refrigerate 30 minutes.

Cut each bar lengthways into three even slices, cut each slice into three lengths. You should have nine lengths from each bar.

Stack alternate flavours of lengths of dough, brushing each length of dough lightly but evenly with egg white as you stack. Start with three lengths, building up to nine lengths in each stack. Wrap each bar in baking paper; refrigerate 30 minutes.

Use a sharp knife to cut bars into 1cm-thick slices; place cut-side-up, about 2cm apart, onto baking-paper-lined oven trays.

Stained–glass lollypops, page 34

Using 1.5cm round cutter, cut out 12 rounds from dough, place about 5cm apart on baking-paper-lined oven trays. Starting from the centres of the cookies, use graduating sized round cutters to cut out lollypop shapes (see recipe). Remove excess dough from lollypops.

Brush dough evenly but lightly with lightly beaten egg white, then sprinkle with hundreds and thousands if you like. Slide a paddle pop stick under the circles of dough to the centre of each lollypop. Proceed with recipe.

Coconut fortune cookies, page 21

Make sure you have all your messages ready. As soon as the cookies are baked, remove them from the oven; quickly slide a knife or spatula blade under each cookie to loosen them, then enclose a message in each.

Quickly position each warm cookie over the rim of a glass for 30 seconds to shape; place on wire racks to cool completely.

Frangipanis, page 77
Using 7cm flower cutter (see page 115), cut out flower shapes from rolled-out dough. Place flowers into lightly greased round-based patty pans (see page 108). Bake as directed in recipe. Cool flowers in pan.

The "Push" test
Most cookies baked on an oven tray should feel a little soft after they've been removed from the oven, they become firm when they cool. If you're in doubt about the firmness, remove the cookies from the oven, then "push" one of the cookies on the tray: if it slides, it's done, if it sticks, it needs more baking.

Paper piping bag
Cut a triangle (with all sides the same length) from greaseproof or baking paper. With the apex of the triangle pointing towards you, twist the triangle into a cone shape, by bringing all three points of the triangle together.

Fold the points over, secure with a staple or sticky tape. Two-thirds fill the bag with icing etc, then fold the top of the bag over to enclose the filling. Snip a tiny piece from the end of the bag ready for piping.

We have used a wide variety of metal cutters, all shapes and sizes, throughout this book. They are available from cake decorator's shops, cookware shops, some department stores and craft shops.

The measurements of the cutters used in the recipes were taken by measuring the longest/widest part of the cutter, for example, we measured a square cutter diagonally.

glossary

After Dinner Mints mint squares coated in dark chocolate.

almond

flaked paper-thin almond slices.

meal also known as ground almonds; nuts are powdered to a coarse flour texture for use in baking or as a thickening agent.

apple juice concentrate the juice is extracted from the fruit, then pasteurised and evaporated under vacuum. Available at health food stores.

baking powder a raising agent consisting mainly of two parts cream of tartar to one part bicarbonate of soda (baking soda).

bicarbonate of soda also known as baking soda.

butter use salted or unsalted ("sweet") butter; 125g is equal to 1 stick of butter.

buttermilk sold alongside fresh milk products in supermarkets and is commercially made, by a method similar to yogurt. Is a good substitute for dairy products such as cream or sour cream.

cachous mini (3mm to 5mm), metallic-looking-but-edible multi-coloured confectionery balls.

chai tea tea drink of India made with a mix of spices such as pepper, cardamom and cinnamon.

Cherry Ripe bars dark chocolate bar made from coconut and cherries; standard size bar weighs 35g

chilli, red thai also known as "scuds"; tiny, very hot and bright red in colour.

chocolate

dark Bits also known as chocolate chips and chocolate morsels.

dark eating made of cocoa liquor, cocoa butter and sugar.

Melts discs made of milk, white or dark compound chocolate; good for melting and moulding.

milk eating most popular eating chocolate, mild and very sweet; similar in make-up to dark with the difference being the addition of milk solids.

white eating contains no cocoa solids, deriving its sweet flavour from cocoa butter. Is very sensitive to heat.

chocolate hazelnut spread also known as Nutella; made of cocoa powder, hazelnuts, sugar and milk.

cocoa powder unsweetened, dried, roasted, ground, cocoa beans.

coconut

desiccated unsweetened, concentrated, dried shredded coconut.

essence synthetically produced from flavouring, oil and alcohol.

shredded unsweetened thin strips of dried coconut flesh.

coffee liqueur an alcoholic syrup distilled from wine or brandy and flavoured with coffee. Use Tia Maria, Kahlua or any generic brand.

condensed milk a canned milk product consisting of milk with more than half the water removed and sugar added.

cornflour also known as cornstarch. Available made from corn or wheat.

craisins dried cranberries packaged like raisins and sultanas and available in supermarkets.

cream cheese known as philadelphia or philly; a soft cow-milk cheese with 14% to 33% fat.

cream (minimum fat content 18%), also known as single cream.

cream of tartar the acid ingredient in baking powder; added to confectionery recipes to prevent sugar crystallising. Keeps frostings creamy and improves volume when beating egg whites.

custard powder instant mixture used to make pouring custard; similar to North American instant pudding mixes.

coloured sprinkles also known as Dollar 5s.

dark rum we prefer to use an underproof rum (not overproof) for a more subtle flavour.

dried currants dried tiny, almost black raisins. These are not the same as fresh currants, which are the fruit of a plant in the gooseberry family.

dried lavender and rose buds available at specialist cooking stores.

eggs recipes may call for raw or barely cooked eggs; exercise caution if there is a salmonella problem in your area, especially in food eaten by children and pregnant women.

food colouring vegetable-based substances in liquid, paste or gel form.

flour

plain also known as all-purpose; unbleached wheat flour.

rice very fine, almost powdery, gluten-free flour; made from ground white rice.

wholemeal plain also called wholewheat flour; milled with the wheatgerm so is higher in fibre and more nutritional than plain flour.

glacé cherries also known as candied cherries; boiled in heavy sugar syrup and then dried.

glacé ginger fresh ginger root preserved in sugar syrup; crystallised ginger can be substituted if rinsed with warm water and dried before use.

glacé pineapple pineapple cooked in heavy sugar syrup then dried.

golden syrup a by-product of refined sugarcane; pure maple syrup or honey can be substituted.

hard caramels confectionery item made from sugar, glucose, condensed milk, flour, oil and gelatine.

hazelnut meal ground hazelnuts.

hundreds and thousands tiny balls of multi-coloured sugar-syrup-coated sugar crystals.

instant latte sachets made by Nestle, caffè latte-flavoured milk powder; available in most supermarkets.

jam preserve or conserve; a thickened mixture of a fruit and sugar.

jelly crystals a combination of sugar, gelatine, colours and flavours; when dissolved in water, the solution sets as firm jelly.

lemon grass a tall, clumping, lemon-smelling and tasting, sharp-edged aromatic tropical grass; the white lower part of the stem is used, finely chopped. Can be found, fresh, dried, powdered and frozen, in supermarkets and greengrocers as well as Asian food shops.

macadamias native to Australia; fairly large, slightly soft, buttery rich nut. Should always be stored in the fridge to prevent their high oil content turning them rancid.

malted milk powder a blend of milk powder and malted cereal extract.

mandarin also known as tangerine; a small, loose-skinned, easy-to-peel, sweet and juicy citrus fruit, prized for its eating qualities more than for juicing.

maple syrup distilled from the sap of maple trees mainly from Canada. Maple-flavoured syrup is not an adequate substitute.

marshmallows made from sugar, glucose, gelatine and cornflour.

marzipan a paste made from ground almonds, sugar and water. Similar to almond paste but sweeter, more pliable and finer in texture. Easily coloured and rolled into thin sheets to cover cakes, or sculpted into shapes for confectionery.

mixed dried fruit a mix of sultanas, raisins, currants, peel and cherries.

mixed peel candied citrus peel.

mixed spice a classic spice mixture generally containing caraway, allspice, coriander, cumin, nutmeg and ginger, although cinnamon and other spices can be added. It is used with fruit and in cakes.

oatbran protective outer coating of oats.

peanut butter a creamy blend of ground peanuts, vegetable oil and salt. Most commonly available smooth or crunchy, in supermarkets

pistachio green, delicately flavoured nuts inside hard off-white shells. Available salted or unsalted in their shells; you can also buy them shelled.

poppy seeds small, dried, bluish-grey seeds of the poppy plant, with a crunchy texture and a nutty flavour. Can be purchased whole or ground from most supermarkets.

prepared fondant also known as soft icing and ready-to-roll.

prunes dried plums.

rhubarb a plant with long, green-red stalks; edible when cooked.

rolled barley sliced barley kernels rolled flat into flakes.

rolled oats flattened oat grain rolled into flakes and traditionally used for porridge. Instant oats are also available, but use traditional oats for baking.

sesame snaps sesame seeds set in honey-toffee; sold in thin bar-shapes. Available from supermarkets.

sugar

brown an extremely soft, fine granulated sugar retaining molasses for its characteristic colour and flavour.

icing also known as confectioners' sugar or powdered sugar; pulverised granulated sugar crushed together with a small amount (about 3 per cent) of cornflour.

palm also known as nam tan pip, jaggery, jawa or gula melaka; made from the sap of the sugar palm tree. Light brown to black in colour and usually sold in rock-hard cakes; use brown sugar if unavailable.

pure icing also called confectioners' sugar or powdered sugar.

sugar-free fruit drops individually wrapped fruit-flavoured hard lollies.

vanilla extract obtained from vanilla beans infused in water; a non-alcoholic version of essence.

vegetable oil extracted from plant sources.

wheat germ embryo of the wheat kernel, separated before milling.

conversion chart

measures

One Australian metric measuring cup holds approximately 250ml; one Australian metric tablespoon holds 20ml; one Australian metric teaspoon holds 5ml.

The difference between one country's measuring cups and another's is within a two- or three-teaspoon variance, and will not affect your cooking results. North America, New Zealand and the United Kingdom use a 15ml tablespoon.

All cup and spoon measurements are level. The most accurate way of measuring dry ingredients is to weigh them. When measuring liquids, use a clear glass or plastic jug with the metric markings.

We use large eggs with an average weight of 60g.

dry measures

METRIC	IMPERIAL
15g	½oz
30g	1oz
60g	2oz
90g	3oz
125g	4oz (¼lb)
155g	5oz
185g	6oz
220g	7oz
250g	8oz (½lb)
280g	9oz
315g	10oz
345g	11oz
375g	12oz (¾lb)
410g	13oz
440g	14oz
470g	15oz
500g	16oz (1lb)
750g	24oz (1½lb)
1kg	32oz (2lb)

liquid measures

METRIC	IMPERIAL
30ml	1 fluid oz
60ml	2 fluid oz
100ml	3 fluid oz
125ml	4 fluid oz
150ml	5 fluid oz (¼ pint/1 gill)
190ml	6 fluid oz
250ml	8 fluid oz
300ml	10 fluid oz (½ pint)
500ml	16 fluid oz
600ml	20 fluid oz (1 pint)
1000ml (1 litre)	1¾ pints

length measures

3mm	⅛in
6mm	¼in
1cm	½in
2cm	¾in
2.5cm	1in
5cm	2in
6cm	2½in
8cm	3in
10cm	4in
13cm	5in
15cm	6in
18cm	7in
20cm	8in
23cm	9in
25cm	10in
28cm	11in
30cm	12in (1ft)

oven temperatures

These oven temperatures are only a guide for conventional ovens. For fan-forced ovens, check the manufacturer's manual.

	°C (CELSIUS)	°F (FAHRENHEIT)	GAS MARK
Very slow	120	250	½
Slow	150	275-300	1-2
Moderately slow	160	325	3
Moderate	180	350-375	4-5
Moderately hot	200	400	6
Hot	220	425-450	7-8
Very hot	240	475	9

index

ARE YOU MISSING SOME OF THE WORLD'S FAVOURITE COOKBOOKS?

The Australian Women's Weekly Cookbooks are available from bookshops, cookshops, supermarkets and other stores all over the world. You can also buy direct from the publisher, using the order form below.

TITLE	RRP	QTY	TITLE	RRP	QTY
Asian Meals in Minutes	£6.99		Japanese Cooking Class	£6.99	
Babies & Toddlers Good Food	£6.99		Just For One	£6.99	
Barbecue Meals In Minutes	£6.99		Kids' Birthday Cakes	£6.99	
Beginners Cooking Class	£6.99		Kids Cooking	£6.99	
Beginners Simple Meals	£6.99		Kids' Cooking Step-by-Step	£6.99	
Beginners Thai	£6.99		Lean Food	£6.99	
Best Food	£6.99		Low-carb, Low-fat	£6.99	
Best Food Desserts	£6.99		Low-fat Feasts	£6.99	
Best Food Fast	£6.99		Low-fat Food For Life	£6.99	
Best Food Mains	£6.99		Low-fat Meals in Minutes	£6.99	
Cafe Classics	£6.99		Main Course Salads	£6.99	
Cakes Biscuits & Slices	£6.99		Mexican	£6.99	
Cakes Cooking Class	£6.99		Middle Eastern Cooking Class	£6.99	
Caribbean Cooking	£6.99		Midweek Meals in Minutes	£6.99	
Casseroles	£6.99		Moroccan & the Foods of North Africa	£6.99	
Casseroles & Slow-Cooked Classics	£6.99		Muffins, Scones & Breads	£6.99	
Cheap Eats	£6.99		New Casseroles	£6.99	
Cheesecakes: baked and chilled	£6.99		New Classics	£6.99	
Chicken	£6.99		New Curries	£6.99	
Chicken Meals in Minutes	£6.99		New Finger Food	£6.99	
Chinese Cooking Class	£6.99		New French Food	£6.99	
Christmas Cooking	£6.99		New Salads	£6.99	
Chocolate	£6.99		Party Food and Drink	£6.99	
Cocktails	£6.99		Pasta Meals in Minutes	£6.99	
Cooking for Friends	£6.99		Potatoes	£6.99	
Cupcakes & Fairycakes	£6.99		Salads: Simple, Fast & Fresh	£6.99	
Detox	£6.99		Saucery	£6.99	
Dinner Beef	£6.99		Sauces Salsas & Dressings	£6.99	
Dinner Lamb	£6.99		Sensational Stir-Fries	£6.99	
Dinner Seafood	£6.99		Slim	£6.99	
Easy Curry	£6.99		Soup	£6.99	
Easy Spanish-Style	£6.99		Stir-fry	£6.99	
Essential Soup	£6.99		Superfoods for Exam Success	£6.99	
Foods That Fight Back	£6.99		Sweet Old-fashioned Favourites	£6.99	
Fresh Food Fast	£6.99		Tapas Mezze Antipasto & other bites	£6.99	
Fresh Food for Babies & Toddlers	£6.99		Thai Cooking Class	£6.99	
Good Food Fast	£6.99		Traditional Italian	£6.99	
Great Lamb Cookbook	£6.99		Vegetarian Meals in Minutes	£6.99	
Greek Cooking Class	£6.99		Vegie Food	£6.99	
Grills	£6.99		Wicked Sweet Indulgences	£6.99	
Healthy Heart Cookbook	£6.99		Wok Meals in Minutes	£6.99	
Indian Cooking Class	£6.99		TOTAL COST:	£	

Mr/Mrs/Ms _____

Address _____

_____ Postcode _____

Day time phone _____ Email* (optional) _____

I enclose my cheque/money order for £ _____

or please charge £ _____

to my: ☐ Access ☐ Mastercard ☐ Visa ☐ Diners Club

PLEASE NOTE: WE DO NOT ACCEPT SWITCH OR ELECTRON CARDS

Card number ☐☐☐☐☐☐☐☐☐☐☐☐☐☐☐☐

Expiry date _____ 3 digit security code *(found on reverse of card)* _____

Cardholder's name_____ Signature _____

To order: Mail or fax – photocopy or complete the order form above, and send your credit card details or cheque payable to: Australian Consolidated Press (UK), Moulton Park Business Centre, Red House Road, Moulton Park, Northampton NN3 6AQ, phone (+44) (0) 1604 497531 fax (+44) (0) 1604 497533, e-mail books@acpuk.com or order online at www.acpuk.com
Non-UK residents: We accept the credit cards listed on the coupon, or cheques, drafts or International Money Orders payable in sterling and drawn on a UK bank. Credit card charges are at the exchange rate current at the time of payment.
Postage and packing UK: Add £1.00 per order plus 50p per book.
Postage and packing overseas: Add £2.00 per order plus £1.00 per book.
All pricing current at time of going to press and subject to change/availability.
Offer ends 31.12.2007

* By including your email address, you consent to receipt of any email regarding this magazine, and other emails which inform you of ACP's other publications, products, services and events, and to promote third party goods and services you may be interested in.